Spiritual

Warfare

Ellis Smiley

TEACH Services, Inc.
PUBLISHING
www.TEACHServices.com • (800) 367-1844

Copyright © 2016 Ellis Smiley

Copyright © 2016 TEACH Services, Inc.

ISBN-13: 978-1-4796-0622-1 (Paperback)
ISBN-13: 978-1-4796-0623-8 (ePub)
ISBN-13: 978-1-4796-0624-5 (Mobi)

Library of Congress Control Number: 2016901763

All Scripture quotations, unless otherwise indicated, are taken from the King James Version.

Scripture quotations marked (NLT) are taken from the Holy Bible, New Living Translation, Copyright © 1996, 2004, 2007 by Tyndale House Foundation. Used by permission of Tyndale House Publishers, Inc., Carol Stream, Illinois 60188. All rights reserved.

Table of Contents

Chapter 1
Fighting the Good Fight

For many years I have struggled with living a victorious Christian life. My Christian life has been like a roller coaster. I would have spiritual highs and spiritual lows and this was extremely frustrating. Some days I just wanted to scream, "*Stop the world and let me get off!* " I would plead to God for answers to stop this up and down spiritual experience. I have yearned for a consistent spiritual walk and have pleaded with God to make this happen in my life.

During my journey for victory, there were days when my mind would get locked onto a certain passage of Scripture and I could not get the Scripture out of my head. I had been thinking about and meditating on Luke 4:18 for about four weeks. I was captivated by the phrase, "He hath sent me to heal the brokenhearted, to preach deliverance to the captives, and recovering sight to the blind..."

One morning as I was waking up, I found myself in a serious conversation with God about this passage of Scripture. "The Spirit of the Lord is upon me, because he hath anointed me to preach the gospel to the poor; he hath sent me to heal the brokenhearted, to preach deliverance to the captives, and recovering of sight to the blind, to set at liberty them that are bruised" (Luke 4:18).

I heard the Holy Spirit say, "Do not move. Do not break what is happening at this moment; be still and see this through." So I waited in bed, allowing God to reveal to me more about this Scripture. After about five minutes of being in prayer about the verse, I asked this question, "God, how am I in captivity and what are You trying to deliver me from?" God said, "Ellis, your mind is hostile toward Me. You act as though I am your enemy."

Then God began to explain the following passages of Scripture to me. "Ye have heard that it hath been said, An eye for an eye, and a tooth for a tooth: But I say unto you, That ye resist not evil: but whosoever shall smite thee on thy right cheek, turn to him the other also" (Matt. 5:38, 39). God said, "Ellis you do not have to get people back when they do you wrong. If someone hits you on the right cheek, then turn to them the left cheek, and do not retaliate." I said, "God, my mind does not work like that." God replied, "That is the problem Ellis. Your mind is at enmity or hostile toward living the way I am asking and have called you to live."

He reminded me of Matthew 5:40–42. "And if any man will sue thee at the law, and take away thy coat, let him have thy cloak also. And whosoever shall compel thee to go a mile, go with him twain. Give to him that asketh thee, and from him that would borrow of thee turn not thou away." My interpretation of the Scripture is that if someone wants to sue me and take away my possessions, let them have them. If they ask me to go a mile, go two miles. If they ask me for a dollar, give them two dollars. Give to anyone that asks, and to those who ask to borrow, do not turn them away. This is so unlike what I have been taught, how I think, or how I operate.

Then I was reminded of Luke 6:35. "But love ye your enemies, and do good, and lend, hoping for nothing again; and your reward shall be great, and ye shall be the children of the Highest: for he is kind unto the unthankful and to the evil." My response was, "Lord, You want me to lend, hoping for nothing again?" Sometimes I don't want to give, yet now You are saying to give and hope for nothing in return. I get tired of people borrowing tools, money, cars, etc. But You are saying do not turn them away; that I should actually give them the things they are asking to borrow and I should not get upset or disappointed if they do not return what they have borrowed.

He next brought to my mind Matthew 5:43, 44. "Ye have heard that it hath been said, Thou shalt love thy neighbour, and hate thine enemy. But I say unto you, Love your enemies, bless them that curse you, do good to them that hate you, and pray for them which despitefully use you, and persecute you." I said to God, "You want me to love my neighbors (those close to me) and also love those that hate me? You want me to bless them that curse me, bless those who wish me harm, do good to those who hate me, and pray for those who despitefully use me? You want me to even pray for those who persecute me?"

Next the Lord reminded me of the following Scripture. "That ye may be the children of your Father which is in heaven: for he maketh his sun to rise on the evil and on the good, and sendeth rain on the just and on the unjust" (Matt. 5:45). He reminded me that I was His child. Just as children naturally reflect the attributes of their parents, my life should be reflecting the attributes of my Father which is in heaven.

Just as children naturally reflect the attributes of their parents, my life should be reflecting the attributes of my Father which is in heaven.

God makes the sun to rise on the evil and on the good and sends rain on the just and on the unjust. God is not kind only to those who love Him. He also provides for those who don't love Him or serve Him. I responded to God that I am nice to people who are nice to me and I speak to people who speak to me. God said, "What is your point?"

Then He reminded me of Matthew 5:46–48. "For if ye love them which love you, what reward have ye? Do not even the publicans the same? And if ye salute your brethren only, what do ye more than others? Do not even the publicans so? Be ye therefore perfect, even as your Father which is in heaven is perfect." God asked me, "Are you happy because you live like sinners? Do you want a reward for living like those who do not know

God? They only speak to people that speak to them and are kind to people who are kind to them. So do you want to be rewarded for that?"

I was reminded of Luke 6:36. "Be ye therefore merciful, as your Father also is merciful." I asked, "So God, is it Your desire for me to be like You?" God said, "Yes I do want you to be like me." I responded, "But I am so different!" Then He took me to Jeremiah 17:9. "The heart is deceitful above all things, and desperately wicked: who can know it?" The Lord reminded me that people who are drowning are desperate. They need and want air, they cannot continue without it, and they will fight to get more air. They have an urgent need to breathe. Lifeguards have to wait until a person stops fighting before they can be rescued. God said, "Ellis that's you; you are desperate for sin. You behave as if what I am requiring of you is going to kill you. You want to continue to do things your own way in selfishness and sin, and some days you fight the changes I want to accomplish in your life. You are desperate to remain in sin—to stay as you are."

God said, "Ellis that's you; you are desperate for sin.

I went to my Bible and read Romans 7:15–25. "For that which I do I allow not: for what I would, that do I not; but what I hate, that do I. If then I do that which I would not, I consent unto the law that it is good. Now then it is no more I that do it, but sin that dwelleth in me. For I know that in me (that is, in my flesh,) dwelleth no good thing: for to will is present with me;

but *how* to perform that which is good I find not. For the good that I would I do not: but the evil which I would not, that I do. Now if I do that I would not, it is no more I that do it, but sin that dwelleth in me. I find then a law, that, when I would do good, evil is present with me. For I delight in the law of God after the inward man: But I see another law in my members, warring against the law of my mind, and bringing me into captivity to the law of sin which is in my members. O wretched man that I am! who shall deliver me from the body of this death? I thank God through Jesus Christ our Lord. So then with the mind I myself serve the law of God; but with the flesh the law of sin."

The passage says, "in me (that is, in my flesh) dwells no good thing", that sin dwells in me, and that evil is present with me. Yet, I delight in what God says. Consequently, I see and experience a war going on within me. This war is going on in my body. It brings me into captivity to the law of sin which is in my members. I fight within myself. I know I should be kind, I know I should be courteous, I know I should be giving, and I know I should be considerate of others. But sometimes, many times, I just don't want to do what I know I should do. Some people I just don't like and that is a problem. My mind knows what is right, but still sometimes I just don't want to do it. There is a war within me, and that is the battle. I realize God has an agenda and so does Satan. Both are appealing to me to choose their side. God tries to reason with my mind. Satan appeals to my natural sinful flesh. The war is on.

I have to admit there are times when I like the flesh. I am so comfortable with the flesh. I have followed the prompting of my flesh all my life; it comes natural.

That is the problem Romans 7:15–25 is addressing. In verse 24, I see that I am that wretched, miserable man and I need to be delivered from the body of this death. My body loves sin, even though I know it is going to destroy me. I know it causes pain. I know what is right. I know it hurts others, and still sometimes I sin anyway. God says that He wants to and needs to deliver me from myself. My body (flesh) likes sin and if God does not intervene, my own body (flesh) is going to lead me to destruction. I am a wretched and miserable man. I sin, then I have regret, disappointment, guilt, unhappiness, shame, and misery, because I often know better. I just gave in to my natural human tendencies and desires. I need deliverance from myself. I need to be changed.

I need deliverance from myself.
I need to be changed.

Do not misunderstand me, I know God forgives me every time I go to Him and ask for forgiveness. But if I do not allow Him to change me — change the way I think, even change the way I feel about sin — then it is just a matter of time before I return to my sinful ways again and again. You can wash a pig, clean him up, and forgive him for wallowing in the mud, but that does not change his mind. Unless you make the pig understand that the mud is not good for him, when given the opportunity it will return to wallow in the mud again.

In Philippians 2:5 Paul wrote, "**Let this mind be in you, which was also in Christ Jesus.**" God says that He wants to give us a mind like Jesus. He wants to change the way we think. He wants to control our

thoughts and thus change our desire. When He changes
the way we think then our behavior will change naturally.

1 Peter 4:1 reads, **"Forasmuch then as Christ
hath suffered for us in the flesh, arm yourselves
likewise with the same mind: for he that hath suffered in the flesh hath ceased from sin."** This Scripture encourages us to arm yourselves, prepare for battle, "likewise with the same mind." God wants to give
us a mind like Christ. Without that, we are unarmed
and unprepared for this spiritual battle. Until I have
the mind of Christ, I will experience defeat after defeat
over and over again. I will always be wretched and miserable.

I cried out to God that I was tired of wallowing in
sin! He reminded me of Luke 4:18 where Jesus informed
His audience that He came to set the captives free. But
it is hard to free people who do not believe or know that
they are in captivity. Maybe that's why He also said He
came to give sight to the blind—the spiritually blind. I
have been blind to my real problem. Praise God I see
the real problem, and it is me. The problem is ME!

Chapter 2
The Beginning

God is aware of the spiritual warfare that we encounter. He addresses the issue and provides the solution. In Romans 7:24 Paul writes, "O wretched man that I am! Who shall deliver me from the body of this death?" I need deliverance from my own body. You see, my eyes like the way sin looks. My ears like the way sin sounds, my mouth likes the way it tastes, my hands like the way it feels, and sometimes I like to say sinful things. However, I do realize that sin can destroy me. I also recognize if I continue to cater to the desires of my sinful flesh, I am going to destroy myself. Yes, I need deliverance from this body. Even though I realize sin is detrimental to me spiritually, my mind has grown accustomed to catering to the wishes and desires of my flesh. My mind does not like saying "no" to whatever my body wants or lusts after. Therefore, sometimes even though my mind realizes it is not good for me, if my body wants it, my mind tries to make it happen. So if the body cries out for some sinful behavior or act, the mind in spite of knowing better, still tries to make it happen. There have been times in my life when I knew better, but chose to do things that I knew were wrong. Oh, I am that wretched man!

When trying to understand how I became like this, I was led to Genesis chapters 1 to 3. Chapters 1 and 2 reveal that mankind was made by God in His image. Adam and Eve were not reared by bad parents. They did not grow up in a bad neighborhood. They did not hang out with bad kids, they were not reared in poverty, or had some unfortunate situation happen to them. They came into existence from the very hand of God Himself.

Well, what went wrong? What led to their downfall? It is recorded in Genesis 3:1–6. "Now the serpent was more subtil than any beast of the field which the Lord God had made. And he said unto the woman, Yea, hath God said, Ye shall not eat of every tree of the garden? And the woman said unto the serpent, We may eat the fruit of the trees of the garden: but of the fruit of the tree which is in the midst of the garden, God hath said, Ye shall not eat of it, neither shall you touch it, lest ye die. And the serpent said unto the woman, Ye shall not surely die: For God doth know that in the day that ye eat thereof, then your eyes shall be opened, and ye shall be as gods, knowing good and evil. And when the woman saw that the tree was good for food, and that it was pleasant to the eyes, and a tree to be desired to make one wise, she took of the fruit thereof, and did eat, and gave also unto her husband with her; and he did eat." Notice Satan's subtle attack — "The serpent said unto the woman". When something is said, the information enters the mind. Where does the information get processed? The information is processed in the brain, the human mind. Whether the information is true or false the mind still has to process the information. So Satan used verbal communication to pass on to Eve false information. Satan attacked God's character and Eve then processed the lies. With misinformation the human mind is under attack.

Satan attacked God's character and Eve then processed the lies. With misinformation the human mind is under attack.

Note the first few words in verse 6, "And when the woman saw that the tree was good for food..." Verses 2 and 3 make it very clear that initially Eve does not think the fruit of this tree is good for food. What changed her thoughts regarding the fruit from those found in verses 2 and 3 to that of verse 6? Eve's mind began processing the false information about God and about the tree. Eve began to believe the lies of Satan instead of the truths that God had told her. Note the phrase "...when the woman saw... " Initially she saw things one way. Then she began to see things differently. Initially she saw things God's way. After her mind processed false information that she received from Satan, Eve then began to see things the serpent's way.

Once Satan influenced how Eve thought, then the playing field changed. Eve's view of the tree then changed. God and Eve no longer see the tree the same. Eve began to see the tree as desirable to make her wise. The definition for desire is to covet, lust, and a longing for that which God has forbidden. Eve started to desire, covet, lust after, and want what the serpent said was possible. Eve began to want and long for that which God had forbidden, the "fruit of the tree which is in the midst of the garden". So Eve "took"—also known as stealing—the fruit and ate it. First, Eve coveted the fruit. Next, she was willing to steal in order to get it, and after that, even if it killed her, she would eat it.

What went wrong? Note 2 Peter 1:4. "...having escaped the corruption that is in the world through lust." Eve listened to Satan's lies and believed them. So, sin enters this world through lust. Eve took the fruit and ate it. Then she gave the fruit to Adam and he ate the fruit also. Now they both had sinned. As mates, they could only reproduce after their kind. As two sinners, they brought sinful children into the world. At that point mankind had joined the war. Mankind had joined Satan's side in the spiritual warfare but God refused to walk away in defeat.

God showed up in the garden looking for Adam and Even to let them know that He had a solution to their situation. In Genesis 3:8-21, God declares that He can fix this problem. He has a remedy. Today the human mind is constantly being bombarded with mis-information and ideas that contradict what God says.

Don't be too hard on Eve,—who have we been listening to ourselves? Do we spend time listening to information that contradicts what *"God hath said"*? We spend time listening to information that definitely did not come from God. When we see things the serpent's way, we take, eat, and covet the things that God has forbidden. We duplicate Eve's behavior. Praise God that He has a remedy!

Chapter 3
It's a Mind Thing

Like Eve, our mind processes all information both good and bad. Therefore, we need to be careful what we allow our minds to dwell on. God has instructed us on what we need to think about. In Philippians 4:8 Paul wrote, "Finally, brethren, whatsoever things are true, whatsoever things are honest, whatsoever things are just, whatsoever things are pure, whatsoever things are lovely, whatsoever things are of good report; if there be any virtue, and if there be any praise, think on these things." What we think about has a major influence on what we do. For example, have you ever watched a commercial about food, and the next thing you know, you are in the kitchen raiding the refrigerator? And you know you have just finished eating less than an hour ago and you are not hungry. Yet, the commercial has influenced or convinced you that you are hungry.

We are instructed in Proverbs 23:7, "For as he thinketh in his heart, so is he." Note the place where the thinking occurs. All of our thinking takes place in our mind. Therefore, when God refers to the "heart", He is talking about the mind. All of my thinking transpires in my mind. Also in Genesis 6:5 we find another example. "And God saw that the wickedness of man was great in the earth, and that every imagination of the thoughts of his heart was only evil continually." The place where imagination and thoughts occur God calls the heart. Thus, God is talking about the mind. Consider Luke 5:22. "But when Jesus perceived their thoughts, he answering said unto them, What reason ye in your hearts?" Here also, the place where thoughts occur Jesus calls the heart. In Matthew 9:4 it reads, "And Jesus knowing their thoughts said, Wherefore think ye evil in your hearts?" Again, Jesus calls the place where thinking occurs "the heart".

Remember what you plant will grow, whether it is good or bad. It is vital in our Christian journey to fill our minds with the Word of God.

In Proverbs 4:23 we find the verse, "Keep thy heart with all diligence; for out of it are the issues of life." God is telling us that we should protect and guard our minds. Do not allow Satan to run all kinds of foolishness through your mind. If you put garbage in, you can only get garbage out. Remember what you plant will grow, whether it is good or bad. It is vital in our Christian journey to fill our minds with the Word of God. We cannot survive this spiritual warfare if we are not armed with the Word of God. God says out of the heart are the issues of life. My mind controls everything. So much of what my life is comes from what is going on in my mind. Eve did not take the fruit from the tree until her mind gave her the green light. By the same token, I don't tell people off until my mind gives me the consent and says let them have it. Therefore, we must diligently guard our minds.

We are told that our behavior comes from the thoughts that are in the mind. Matthew 15:19 reads, "For out of the heart proceed evil thoughts, murders, adulteries, fornications, thefts, false witness, blasphemies." Before the body performs the act, the mind has already given approval. Sometimes it happens so fast you can't even keep up. Have you ever cursed someone before you realized what you were saying or snapped at someone without even thinking? Your mind is quick. This is why it is crucial to put God's Word in our minds daily so that God can change our thoughts and thus our actions. God wants us to be consistent in our walk. Eve was drawn to the tree by the talking serpent, she believed the lies of Satan, and lusted after the fruit. In James 1:14, 15 it reads, "But every man is tempted, when he is drawn away of his own lust, and enticed. Then when lust hath conceived, it bringeth forth sin: and sin, when it is finished, bringeth forth death." Satan put thoughts in Eve's mind and she began to see the tree and God's instructions differently. Satan drew her mind away and he draws our minds away from God's will. He watches our lives to see what we like, then presents the opportunity for us to indulge in it by means that contradict what God says. Notice the word "entice". Satan cannot force you to sin, he can only entice. He wants to make sin look inviting and appealing. A fisherman cannot force fish to take the bait. However, he tries to make the bait appear to be simply irresistible and draw the fish away from the place of safety. Satan tries to draw you away, enticing you. When I spend time thinking about, watching and listening to sinful things, then doing them becomes really easy. There are times after thinking about, watching, listening, and dwelling on sin it is just a matter of time before I perform that very sin. That is why we are counseled to follow the words of 2 Corinthians 10:5: "Casting down imaginations, and every high thing that exalteth itself against the knowledge of God, and bringing into captivity every thought to the obedience of Christ." This Scripture also reminds me that there are things in my mind that need to be cast down. There are things in my mind that are against the knowledge of God and those thoughts need to be brought into captivity to the obedience of Christ.

You are responsible to God for the indulgence of vain thoughts; for from vain imaginations arises the committal of sins.

I must be intentional about what I allow to enter my mind. We are encouraged to control our thoughts. "It is your duty to control your thoughts. You will have to war against a vain imagination. You may think that there can be no sin in permitting your thoughts to run as they naturally would without restraint. But this is not so. You are responsible to God for the indulgence of vain thoughts; for from vain imaginations arises the committal of sins, the actual doing of those things upon which the mind has dwelt. Govern your thoughts, and it will then be much easier to govern your actions."[1] Could it be by controlling on what I allow my mind to dwell, my actions would be more in harmony with God? If I spend more time in the Word of God than on other distractions such as watching television, surfing the internet, and being with ungodly friends, could I have victory over the thing that so easily besets me?

We are told that all, including ministers, are in a spiritual warfare and that it is our duty to resist the enemy. "I saw that ministers, as well as people, have a warfare before them, to resist the Devil. It is a cruel position for ministering brethren to be in, serving the purposes of Satan, by listening to his whisperings, and letting him captivate their minds and guide their thoughts."[2] We must guard our minds. "Neither yield ye your members as instruments of unrighteousness unto sin: but yield yourselves unto God, as those that are alive from the dead, and your members as instruments of righteousness unto God" (Rom. 6:13). The word "yield" means to end resistance, to surrender, to relinquish control to the physical control of another. So God is asking me to allow Him to control my life, to trust Him to run things for me. I cannot trust my own mind because it is deceitful and desperately wicked. I must surrender to God daily in this spiritual battle.

We can not control the thoughts that enter our minds; therefore, we must bring all of our thoughts into obedience to Christ. I must cast down those thoughts that are not of God and choose to dwell on those things that are of God. "And supper being ended, the devil having now put into the heart of Judas Iscariot, Simon's son, to betray him" (John 13:2). Note who put it into Judas' heart to betray Jesus. It is dangerous to trust every thought that is going on in my mind because, like Judas, some things are definitely not from God. "But Peter said, Ananias, why hath Satan filled thine heart to lie to the Holy Ghost, and to keep back part of the price of the land?" (Acts 5:3). Satan filled Ananias' heart to lie. So apparently it is not safe for me to trust my own heart or mind.

Now I no longer fear what will happen here on planet Earth in these last days. I am more afraid of the foolishness going on in my own mind. My heart is deceitful and desperately wicked. I need God to deliver me from the foolishness of my own mind. I know He loves me. But still some days I don't want to relinquish control. Some days I do not want to surrender to Him and do things His way. I think, *I've got this.* Yes, Jesus came to set the captives free, but I have been in captivity so long that I now am afraid of freedom. I know sin, I do it without even thinking. But choosing righteousness, turning the other cheek, yielding to the Holy Spirit, being kind and merciful, and forgiving others — that's another story. That is not natural. That is not what I am accustomed to doing.

Chapter 4
God's Answer

This spiritual warfare is a battle that is fought daily. We need God to lead and guide us as we engage in the battle. Proverbs 3: 5–7 encourages us to, "Trust in the LORD with all thine heart; and lean not unto thine own understanding. In all thy ways acknowledge Him, and He shall direct thy paths. Be not wise in thine own eyes: fear the LORD, and depart from evil." Let's break down these verses so we can understand what God is saying to us. When we trust God we "put our confidence in, or sure hope" in Him. We know that the heart is the "mind or intelligence". We are encouraged not to lean, "to rely on, to support oneself", but instead to acknowledge or to "recognize, be aware of, and consider" Him. I need to put my confidence in the Lord with all my mind

and intelligence and lean not unto my own understanding. It is not safe for me to rely upon my own reasoning
because my mind is not trustworthy. In all my ways, I
need to acknowledge, recognize, consider, and be aware
of God. If I acknowledge Him in all actions, God has
promised that He will direct my path. "Be not wise in
thine own eyes: fear the LORD, and depart from evil"
(Prov. 3:7). To fear God in this passage is to "reverence"
Him. The fear of the Lord has nothing to do with super-
stition and fear of divine punishment. Instead it should
be understood as the acute consciousness of God's personal presence at all times and everywhere. When I was
a child, out of respect for my parents, there were some
things I would not do or say in their presence. What
would happen if we began to live with an acute consciousness of God's personal presence and a realization
that we are constantly in His presence? Consequently,
with the acute awareness that I am in the presence of
God, there are some things that I would not do or say.
Realizing that everything I do, everywhere I go, God is
with me. This would change the way I live daily.

Proverbs 15:3 reads, "The eyes of the LORD are
in every place, beholding the evil and the good". God
is everywhere. He is aware of everything in the universe and in my life. In Genesis 17:1, God was talking
to Abram and said to him "...I am the Almighty God;
walk before me, and be thou perfect". The word "walk"
here means to "behave yourself". The words "before me"
means "in my presence". So God is saying to Abram,
"Behave yourself and live as if you are in My presence."
God is asking the same of us today. He wants us to live
as though we are in His very presence; as though He is
right beside us. What an impact this would have on our

lives if we would begin to behave ourselves and live as if we're in the very presence of God daily! This would change some of the places we go, some of our entertainment, some of the words that come out of our mouths, and truly the way that we live.

God wants us to give Him our minds. In Proverbs 23:26 we read, "My son, give me thine heart, and let thine eyes observe my ways". He promises us, "Thou wilt keep him in perfect peace, whose mind is stayed on thee: because he trusteth in thee"(Isa. 26:3).

> "For who hath known the mind of the Lord, that he may instruct him? but we have the mind of Christ" (1 Cor. 2:16).

> "Let this mind be in you, which was also in Christ Jesus" (Phil. 2:5).

> "If so be that ye have heard him, and have been taught by him, as the truth is in Jesus: That ye put off concerning the former conversation the old man, which is corrupt according to the deceitful lusts: and be renewed in the spirit of your mind" (Eph. 4:21–23).

God wants to renew our minds.

> "That Christ may dwell in your hearts by faith; that ye, being rooted and grounded in love" (Eph. 3:17).

> "...God is love" (1 John 4:8).

God wants us to be rooted and grounded in Him.

> "In whom ye also are builded together for an habitation of God through the Spirit" (Eph 2:22). In each of

these passages God addresses the importance of allowing Him to impact our minds. Remember God promised
Adam and Eve that He can fix this sin problem. The
core of man's problem is the human mind. We do not
think the way God thinks. Our thoughts are selfish and
evil. God is trying to fix our thoughts. Man's heart is
desperately wicked and God is desperately trying to
restore His image in us. God is not happy with what sin
has done to mankind. The results of sin in His creation
saddens God greatly.

---

*We do not think the way God thinks.
Our thoughts are selfish and evil.
God is trying to fix our thoughts.*

Someone once told me that God was not seeking
weekend visitation rights. He wants sole custody. He
wants to dwell in us and have us grounded in Him. God
says we were built to be the place where He dwells.

Evil thoughts destroy the soul. The converting
power of God changes the heart, refining and
purifying the thoughts. Unless a determined
effort is made to keep the thoughts centered
on Christ, grace cannot reveal itself in the
life. The mind must engage in the spiritual
warfare. Every thought must be brought into
captivity to the obedience of Christ. All the
habits must be brought under God's control. [3]

We should think of what we are to Jesus,
and of what he is to us, that we may carry
on a successful warfare against the flesh, and

against the natural tendencies of the mind.
We are exhorted to gird up the loins of the
mind, and to do this we must settle the mind
upon Jesus.[4]

It is by the Spirit that the heart (mind) is
made pure. Through the Spirit the believer
becomes a partaker of the divine nature.
Christ has given his Spirit as a divine power
to overcome all hereditary and cultivated tendencies to evil, and to impress his own character upon the church.[5] (Clarification added).

God wants to impress His character upon the people,
not the physical building called the church.

At the cost of infinite sacrifice and suffering,
Christ has provided for us every essential to
success in the Christian warfare. The Holy
Spirit brings power that enables man to overcome. It is through the agency of the Spirit that
the government of Satan is to be subdued. It is
the Spirit that convinces of sin, and, with the
consent of the human being, expels sin from
the heart. The mind is then brought under a
new law,—the royal law of liberty.[6]

"The carnal mind is enmity against God; for it
is not subject to the law of God, neither indeed
can be." Therefore there is a constant warfare
between inclination and duty. Inclination too
often prevails, and silences the convictions of
the Holy Spirit.[7]

"Be transformed by the renewing of your
mind" (Rom. 12: 1, 2).

Chapter 5
Deliverance

There are days when we spend so much time focused on the physical side of life that we overlook the spiritual side of things. Allow me to give an example. The book of Exodus gives an account of God's deliverance of the children of Israel out of Egyptian bondage. From the beginning of God's encounter with Moses, to their actual crossing of the Red Sea, is a matter of weeks or perhaps months. So it did not take long for God to deliver them out of the physical bondage of Egypt. But God spent the next forty years trying to get Egypt out of the people.

When they experienced deliverance from Pharaoh, the Israelites were just as happy as they could be. However, God wanted them to experience restoration as

well. Deliverance from sin and restoration to His image
was God's plan for them. You see, God had a Promised
Land for the people; now He was trying to prepare the
people for the Promised Land. "But with many of them
God was not well pleased: for they were overthrown in
the wilderness. Now these things were our examples,
to the intent that we should not lust (desire) after evil
things, as they also lusted (desired)" (1 Cor. 10:5, 6).
(Clarification added.) God intended that when they
arrived in this Promised Land the Israelites would con-
duct themselves in a godly or righteous manner. They
would live like children of God and their lives would
reflect His character, His principles, and His values.

"Now all these things happened unto them for
examples: and they are written for our admonition,
upon whom the ends of the world are come. Wherefore
let him that thinketh that he standeth take heed lest
he fall" (1 Cor. 10:11, 12). With that in mind, I understand it is not safe for me to be content with deliverance
and forgiveness only. I need restoration as well. Genesis
1:26, 27 tells us that man was made in the image of God,
after His likeness. In Luke 3:38 Adam is referred to as
the son of God. God was his Father. The One responsible for his existence.

Remember after Israel's deliverance there were
times when they missed Egypt, and if God had not
intervened some would have returned to Egypt. Why
did they want to return? They missed the onions, leeks,
and the garlic. They felt at home in Egypt. This is where
they were born, where they were reared and grew up.
They were very comfortable with Egypt, but knew that
there was something better in the land that God had
promised to their forefathers. I sometimes find myself

acting like the Israelites. I was born in sin, grew up in sin, and am comfortable committing sin. Some days I find myself reminiscing about my sinful past. But like the Israelites, I know that God has something better.

Deliverance was great, it was exciting, and it was what the Israelites had prayed for. However, restoration requires sacrifice. It required them to give up some of the things that they liked. It required them to change their behavior and to embrace some things that they were not accustomed to. If they were to be restored to God's image, change must happen, and they were not happy about that. Some days I, too, do not like change. I am not comfortable or familiar with where God is leading me. Like Israel, I have questions about the promised land. I hear that there are giants in the Promised Land and it makes me anxious. Restoration is the process of restoring me to God's image. Consider His image. He is forgiving, loving, kind, He gives even if He gets nothing in return, and He does not remind people of their mistakes. He loves people who do not love Him. God is leading me to unfamiliar territory. "But as many as received him (Jesus), to them gave he power to become the sons of God, even to them that believe on his name" (John 1:12). (Clarification added.)

Children naturally reflect the traits and attributes of their parents. God wanted Israel to reflect His character. This is what He was trying to accomplish. God's plan for Christians today is still the same. He wants to restore our lives so that we again reflect His character. Note the phrase in John 1:12, "to them gave He power to become sons of God". From where does that power come? From the Holy Spirit.

"And hope maketh not ashamed; because the love of God is shed abroad in our hearts by the Holy Ghost which is given unto us" (Rom. 5:5). So the Holy Ghost puts God's love in our hearts. Ephesians 2:22 says you were built to be inhabited by God through the Spirit. Mary, the mother of Jesus, when she asked how a virgin could give birth was told the Holy Ghost would come upon her. God would put this new divine life in her, if she was willing. "The warfare against self is the greatest battle that was ever fought.

The warfare against self is the greatest battle that was ever fought.

The yielding of self, surrendering all to the will of God, requires a struggle; but the soul must submit to God before it can be renewed in holiness." [8] Mary's response was to tell the angel in effect, "I am the servant of the Lord, let God do to my life as seems good in His sight". Are you willing, like Mary, to surrender to God's plan and tell Him that today? Are you willing to allow Him to put a new life in you?

Others may not understand this new life that they see in you. But like Mary, you will know. There was a time when Joseph considered putting Mary away privately. He did not understand what God was doing in her life. So God had to intervene. He sent an angel to Joseph to give him clarity regarding the new life growing in Mary. If Joseph had followed the natural tendencies of his flesh or human emotions, Mary would have been put away.

Evil thoughts destroy the soul. The converting power of God changes the heart, refining and purifying the thoughts. Unless a determined effort is made to keep the thoughts centered on Christ, grace cannot reveal itself in the life. The mind must engage in the spiritual warfare. *Every thought* must be brought into captivity to the obedience of Christ. All the habits must be brought under God's control. We need a constant sense of the ennobling power of pure thoughts and the damaging influence of evil thoughts. Let us place our thoughts upon holy things. Let them be pure and true; for the only security for any soul is right-thinking. We are to use every means that God has placed within our reach for the government and cultivation of our thoughts. We are to bring our minds into harmony with Christ's mind. His truth will sanctify us, body, soul, and spirit, and we shall be enabled to rise above temptation.[9] (Italics added.)

Every thought must be brought into captivity to the obedience of Christ. All the habits must be brought under God's control.

Even in our own lives we cannot safely follow the natural tendencies of our human emotions. Our thoughts, like Joseph's, must be brought into subjection unto the obedience of Christ.

You do not have to follow your own way, to
plan and devise in your own wisdom; if you did,
you would certainly fail. But place yourself as
a learner in Christ's school. He will teach you;
he will discipline and train you in his manner
of working. And the Comforter will bring all
things to your remembrance. You will find, as
you submit to the educating process, that you
are becoming spiritually efficient. Even your
memory will be strengthened.[10]

The children of Israel were, when following their
natural tendencies so often led into some form of disobe-
dience. This is why it was necessary for God to restore
Israel to His image. If they were left to themselves they
would return to wrong behaviors.

God is not just trying to change what you did
wrong, that is, through forgiveness, He is also trying to
change who you are and your future behavior. He wants
to put His divine nature in you. 2 Peter 1:4 says that
"Whereby are given unto us exceeding great and precious promises: that by these ye might be partakers of
the divine nature." Remember He put divinity in Mary
and He wants to do the same for you and me. God wants
to make us partakers of His divine nature. So that we,
"...no longer should live the rest of his (our) time in the
flesh to the lusts (desires) of men, but to the will of God"
(1 Peter 4:2). (Clarification added.). Mary lived to do
God's will. What are you willing to live for?

The warfare in which we are engaged is
largely mental, and the mind that is the most
thoroughly trained will do the most acceptable work...The servants of Christ should

seek to understand the requirements for this time. The conditions of warfare are not what they were years ago, because increased light has been shining upon us, and great and solemn warnings have come to us. Unless we have an understanding of the times in which we live, we may, even with the best of intentions, make great mistakes, and stand in the way of the advancement of the work. The claims upon the Christians are the same now as ever,—perfect obedience,—but Satan's attacks are more deceptive. His manner of warfare is so different from that expected that, unless the senses are sharpened to comprehend his plans, we shall not be prepared for defense.[11]

Satan's ...manner of warfare is so different from that expected that, unless the senses are sharpened to comprehend his plans, we shall not be prepared for defense.

Many times in spite of my good intentions, I have followed the promptings of my flesh and have made terrible mistakes. I was in a spiritual war and did not realize it.

In closing this chapter, I am reminded that in heaven the streets are paved with gold. The gates are made of pearls. The foundation of the city is made of diamonds, gems, and many other precious stones. I wondered why God gave us this information. The answer He impressed me with blew me away. In heaven, those things — gold, pearls, diamonds, etc. — are used as construction material. They have no great value. In heaven those things are used the way we use dirt, sand, wood, asphalt, and gravel. What heaven values is a character that reflects Christ, showing love, kindness, and compassion to others. This character is developed here on earth before we reach heaven; the promised land. May our daily response to God be like that of Mary, "Be it unto me according to thy word."

Chapter 6

Prepare for War

We are in a spiritual battle. However, this is not a physical battle that we are fighting. "For though we walk in the flesh, we do not war after the flesh: (For the weapons of our warfare are not carnal, but mighty through God to the pulling down of strong holds;)" (2 Cor. 10:3, 4). Here God clearly states that we are engaged in warfare. So what are mighty weapons that can pull down strong holds? They are not carnal or physical weapons, but they are mighty through God.

"Forasmuch then as Christ hath suffered for us in the flesh, arm yourselves likewise with the same mind: for he that hath suffered in the flesh hath ceased from sin" (1 Peter 4:1). Arm yourselves with the same mind as Christ. What was the mind of Christ? Jesus was not

here to do His own will, but to do the will of His Father.
"For I came down from heaven, not to do mine own will,
but the will of him that sent me" (John 6:38). "I can of
mine own self do nothing: as I hear, I judge: and my
judgment is just; because I seek not mine own will, but
the will of the Father which hath sent me" (John 5:30).
Jesus came not to be served, but to serve others. The
New Testament is full of examples of Him serving and
caring for the needs of others. "Even as the Son of man
came not to be ministered unto, but to minister, and to
give his life a ransom for many" (Matt. 20:28). So He
came to serve others and to give His life as a ransom for
many. Even when dying on the cross Jesus made sure
that His mother would be cared for after His death by
asking John, His disciple, to care for His mother. Jesus
gave up the riches of heaven, embraced poverty, and
the limitations of a human body so that we, through
His grace, may become rich. "For ye know the grace of
our Lord Jesus Christ, that, though he was rich, yet for
your sakes he became poor, that ye through his poverty might be rich" (2 Cor. 8:9). He willingly laid down
His life to save us. "Therefore doth my Father love me,
because I lay down my life, that I might take it again.
No man taketh it from me, but I lay it down of myself.
I have power to lay it down, and I have power to take
it again. This commandment have I received of my
Father" (John 10:17, 18).

> The Saviour's life on earth was not a life of
> ease and devotion to Himself, but He toiled
> with persistent, earnest, untiring effort for
> the salvation of lost mankind... (Jesus) said,
> "The Son of man came not to be ministered

unto, but to minister, and to give His life a ransom for many." Matthew 20:28. This was the one great object of His life. Everything else was secondary and subservient. It was His meat and drink to do the will of God and to finish His work. Self and self-interest had no part in His labor... So those who are the partakers of the grace of Christ will be ready to make any sacrifice, that others for whom He died may share the heavenly gift. They will do all they can to make the world better for their stay in it. This spirit is the sure out-growth of a soul truly converted.[12]

So when I look at the life of Christ this is what I see. Someone who came:

❖ Not to do His own will but the will of His Father.

❖ Not to be served but to serve others.

❖ To voluntarily lay down His life for others.

❖ To become poor that others may be rich.

❖ To forego His privileges, for the wellbeing of others.

Philippians 2:5 reads, "Let this mind be in you, which was also in Christ Jesus."

Let this mind be in you, which was also in Christ Jesus.

Do not overlook the word "let". God wants to give me the mind of Christ. I must be willing to "let", or allow, God to do this in me. How do I let God do this? I must say "no" to my selfish nature and choose to yield to God's will for my life. I must trust that He knows what is best for me. It does not matter how crucifying it seems to my flesh. I must deny myself and take up my cross and follow Him. I must choose to let God do it. Philippians 1:6 reads, "Being confident of this very thing, that he which hath begun a good work in you will perform it until the day of Jesus Christ." So apparently God wants to make us like Christ. God wants to make this happen. If this is not occurring in me, it is because my flesh does not want to cooperate with God. This is why I need to be delivered from my sinful and selfish human nature.

"Then said Jesus to them again, Peace be unto you: as my Father hath sent me, even so send I you. And when he had said this, he breathed on them, and saith unto them, Receive ye the Holy Ghost" (John 20:21, 22). So, for what purpose was Jesus sent?
Jesus was sent to:

- ❖ bless others

- ❖ serve others

- ❖ enhance the quality of others' walk with God

- ❖ become poor that others may become rich

- ❖ help others get to know the Father's love

- ❖ help the poor, the crippled, the blind, and the unfortunate that they may know that God loves them and has not forgotten them

❖ lay aside His privileges, that the lives of others may be improved

This was God's way of showing the world His love for them. He sends us, as He sent Jesus, to bless and serve others. This is the gospel of Jesus Christ of which Paul says, "I am not ashamed" (Rom. 1:16). The real beauty of the gospel is not just that God loves you. The true beauty of the gospel is demonstrated when I love you like God loves you.

The true beauty of the gospel is demonstrated when I love you like God loves you.

Again, as Paul stated, "For I am not ashamed of the gospel of Christ: for it is the power of God unto salvation to every one that believeth; to the Jew first, and also to the Greek" (Rom. 1:16). I should not be ashamed to serve others, for that is God's way of loving them as well as restoring me, so that my life will reflect His.

And the effort to bless others will react in blessings upon ourselves. This was the purpose of God in giving us a part to act in the plan of redemption. He has granted men the privilege of becoming partakers of the divine nature and, in their turn, of diffusing blessings to their fellow men.[13]

God could have achieved the spread of the gospel without man's assistance. But this was not His plan.

God might have committed the message of the gospel, and all the work of loving ministry, to the heavenly angels. He might have employed other means for accomplishing His purpose. But in His infinite love He chose to make us co-workers with Himself, with Christ and the angels, that we might share the blessing, the joy, the spiritual uplifting, which results from this unselfish ministry.[14]

Our work in this world is to live for others' good, to bless others, to be hospitable; and frequently it may be only at some inconvenience that we can entertain those who really need our care and the benefit of our society and our homes. Some avoid these necessary burdens.[15]

God wants man to get involved in serving others. When we do this—serve others—we stop focusing on ourselves and seek the good of others.

The life that Christ lived was to serve others. If we are going to fight this spiritual war we need to be armed with the mind of Christ. We need to think of others and their needs and seek to do them good.

It is in doing Christ's work that the church has the promise of His presence. Go teach all nations, He said; "and, lo, I am with you alway, even unto the end of the world." To take His yoke is one of the first conditions of receiving His power. The very life of the church depends upon her faithfulness in fulfilling the Lord's commission. To neglect this work is surely to invite spiritual feebleness and decay. Where there is no active labor for others, love wanes, and faith grows dim.[16]

God's law is the law of love. He has surrounded you with beauty to teach you that you are not placed on earth merely to delve for self, to dig and build, to toil and spin, but to make life bright and joyous and beautiful with the love of Christ—like the flowers, to gladden other lives by the ministry of love.[17]

"But ye are a chosen generation, a royal priesthood, an holy nation, a peculiar people; that ye should shew forth the praises of him who hath called you out of darkness into his marvellous light" (1 Peter 2:9). As a royal priesthood, the priests were called to serve others. They lived to serve God and others; not themselves.

Without the mind of Christ, I am just another selfish, self-centered, self-absorbed church member. That kind of life does not reflect Christ or the kingdom of God.

To prepare for war I must allow God to give me the mind of Christ. I must have a new way of thinking and a new way of living. "Forasmuch then as Christ hath suffered for us in the flesh, arm yourselves likewise with the same mind" (1 Peter 4:1). Without the mind of Christ, I am unarmed and no threat to the kingdom of Satan. Without the mind of Christ, I am just another selfish, self-centered, self-absorbed church member.

That kind of life does not reflect Christ or the kingdom of God. With the mind of Christ, I am led by the Holy Spirit and my behavior reflects Christ's character. Self is no longer the center of my world.

Let's face it, selfishness is no threat to Satan's kingdom. That is how sin entered the world. Eve was trying to serve self by taking the fruit. Satan told her what the fruit would do for self —make her like God— and she, unfortunately, believed the lie.

Chapter 7
God's Instructions

Many people are familiar with the contents of God's law, but do not know how to keep it. The law is not to be a checklist we use to see how close we are to God's kingdom; instead, it is to be an instrument that expresses various principles of love. For example, you don't steal from those you love, you don't kill them, or lie to them. Why? Because you love them. Fulfilling the law does not mean we obey it to gain personal favor with God, but it beckons each Christian to share the love of God with those in need.

Read Luke 10:25-37. To paraphrase: The lawyer asked Jesus, "Master what shall I do to inherit eternal life?" Jesus responded, "What is written in the law? How readest thou?" The lawyer answering said, "Thou shall love the Lord thy God with all thy heart, with all thy soul, with all thy strength and with all thy mind, and thy neighbor as thyself." Jesus responded saying, Thou has answered right; this do, and thou shall live". But the lawyer tried to justify himself. Why did he think he needed to justify himself? Because as a Jew, there were some people he did not love, i.e. the Romans, the Gentiles, or the Samaritans. So he wanted to justify to Jesus there were some people that he did not need to love as he loved himself. So he asked Jesus, "Who is my neighbor?"

According to the lawyer's answer in verse 27 and Jesus' response in verse 28, the law teaches that I should love God with all my heart and love others as I love myself. So the real issue for the lawyer was that there are some people he did not love the way he loved himself. Therefore, the question, "Who is my neighbor?" really meant, "Who should I love?" Then Jesus preceded to tell the story of the Good Samaritan. Jesus asked the question, "Which now of these three, thinkest thou, was neighbor unto him that fell among the thieves?" (Luke 10:36). In other words, which one of these loved the man who had fallen among thieves the way he loved himself? Which one was keeping the law, "Love thy neighbor as thyself"?

When I see those who have fallen among thieves—who have been stripped, wounded, left behind, and are less fortunate than myself—if all I do is look on and then pass by them on the other side, I am *not* keeping the law. I am *not* loving them the way I love myself. If I am in an unfortunate situation, I would want someone to do something to change my situation. If someone we love is in an unfortunate situation, we do not just pass them by unless we, like the lawyer, want to justify ourselves. There are times that we, like the lawyer, try to justify why we do not love certain people. We come up with all types of reasons why we do not stop to assist people in need. Of the three people in the story, the Priest, the Levite, and the Samaritan, which one of them reflected Christ's behavior?

Of the three people in the story, the Priest, the Levite, and the Samaritan, which one of them reflected Christ's behavior?

Only the Samaritan loved the man who had fallen among thieves the way he loved himself.

This Samaritan, said Christ, was neighbor to him who fell among thieves. The Levite and the priest represent a class in the church who manifest an indifference to the very ones who need their sympathy and help. This class, notwithstanding their position in the church, are commandment breakers. The Samaritan represents a class who are true helpers with Christ, and who are imitating His example of doing good. Those who have pity for the unfortunate, the blind, the lame, the afflicted, the widows, the orphans, and the needy, Christ represents as commandment keepers, who shall have eternal life... Christ regards all acts of mercy, benevolence, and thoughtful consideration for the unfortunate, the blind, the lame, the sick, the widow, and the orphan as done to Himself; and these works are preserved in the heavenly records and will be rewarded. On the other hand, a record will be written in the book against those who manifest the indifference of the priest and the Levite to the unfortunate, and those who take any advantage of the misfortunes of others, and increase their affliction in order to selfishly advantage themselves. God will surely repay every act of injustice, and every manifestation of careless indifference to and neglect of the afflicted among us. Every one will finally be rewarded as his works have been.[18]

Love is the greatest gift that we can give to God and man. It is by loving God that we experience true love and learn how to really love our fellow man. "Owe no man any thing, but to love one another: for he that loveth another hath fulfilled the law. For this, Thou shalt not commit adultery, Thou shalt not kill, Thou shalt not steal, Thou shalt not bear false witness, Thou shalt not covet; and if there be any other commandment, it is briefly comprehended in this saying, namely, Thou shalt love thy neighbour as thyself. Love worketh no ill to his neighbour: therefore love is the fulfilling of the law" (Rom. 13:8–10). The commandments remind us how love behaves toward others. Therefore, to love others as we love ourselves is keeping the law.

When we love others we are fulfilling the law. Therefore, I show honor and respect to those that I love (fifth commandment). I do not kill those that I love (sixth commandment). Instead, my love for them leads me to protect them. I do not steal from those that I love (seventh commandment). Instead, I add to their lives, not take from them. I do not to commit adultery with or against those I love (eighth commandment). Instead I protect their relationships. I choose not to bear false witness against those I love (ninth commandment). Instead, I want to protect the reputation of the lives of others. Also, I choose not to covet the things that belong to those I love (tenth commandment). Instead, I rejoice that God has blessed them. Therefore, loving others leads to living in harmony with what the law requires. Loving others the way I love myself, I do not want to cause pain and suffering. Instead I seek to protect them, their relationships, and their possessions. Love is the fulfilling of the law.

Loving others the way I love myself, I do not want to cause pain and suffering. Instead I seek to protect them, their relationships, and their possessions.

I, like the lawyer, need to stop trying to justify not loving some people. We are told, in 1 John 4:20, "If a man say, I love God, and hateth his brother, he is a liar: for he that loveth not his brother whom he hath seen, how can he love God whom he hath not seen?" "Hereby perceive we the love of God, because he laid down his life for us: and we ought to lay down our lives for the brethren. But whoso hath this world's good, and seeth his brother have need, and shutteth up his bowels of compassion from him, how dwelleth the love of God in him? My little children, let us not love in word, neither in tongue; but in deed and in truth" (1 John 3:16–18). "He that loveth not knoweth not God; for God is love" (1 John 4:8). "Beloved, if God so loved us, we ought also to love one another" (1 John 4:11). God is calling us to love others the way we love ourselves. The commandments remind us of how love behaves toward others. So God is clearly saying if you love Me you will love others. "If ye love me, keep my commandments"(John 14:15).

Often we look at the law incorrectly. The law reminds me how I am to behave toward others. When I am loving to others, I am fulfilling the law. "When those who profess to serve God follow Christ's example, practicing the principles of the law in their daily life; when every act bears witness that they love God supremely and their neighbor as themselves, then will the church have power to move the world."[19]

Are you ready to move the world for Jesus? If so, love others the way you love yourself.

Chapter 8
Saved to Served

We are invited to present our bodies to God as a living sacrifice, and this is considered our reasonable service. "I beseech you therefore, brethren, by the mercies of God, that ye present your bodies a living sacrifice, holy, acceptable unto God, which is your reasonable service" (Rom. 12:1). In the Old Testament, once the sacrifice was presented to God, the person who brought the sacrifice no longer owned it. The person no longer called the shots as to what happened to the sacrifice. The sacrifice was not taken back home; it was God's possession. Note that God wants a living sacrifice not a dead sacrifice. When I consider His mercies, I now offer myself to Him; this is reasonable and sensible service. My hands, feet, eyes, mouth, and ears now become God's to do His

bidding, His work, and His will. The definition of service in Romans 12:1 is worship. So giving myself to God
as a living sacrifice, where He now calls the shots in my
life, is an act of worship. This is our reasonable service.
In Matthew 25:34–39 Jesus said He had been
hungry, thirsty, a stranger, sick, naked, and in prison,
and the hearers had met His needs. The people asked
Jesus when had He been hungry, thirsty, sick, naked,
and in prison? In verse 40 Jesus responded. "And the
King shall answer and say unto them, Verily I say unto
you, Inasmuch as ye have done it unto one of the least
of these my brethren, ye have done it unto me." So when
we are meeting the needs of the less fortunate, God con-
siders that as serving Him. This is reasonable because
my hands are now His. God wants to use us to minister
to others.

I saw that it is in the providence of God that
widows and orphans, the blind, the deaf,
the lame, and persons afflicted in a variety
of ways, have been placed in close Christian relationship to His church; it is to prove
His people and develop their true character.
Angels of God are watching to see how we
treat these persons who need our sympathy,
love, and disinterested benevolence. This is
God's test of our character. If we have the
true religion of the Bible, we shall feel that a
debt of love, kindness, and interest is due to
Christ in behalf of His brethren; and we can
do no less than to show our gratitude for His
immeasurable love to us while we were sinners unworthy of His grace, by having a deep

interest and unselfish love for those who are our brethren, and who are less fortunate than ourselves.[20]

Loving others is more than just talk. "Hereby perceive we the love of God, because he laid down his life for us: and we ought to lay down our lives for the brethren. But whoso hath this world's good, and seeth his brother have need, and shutteth up his bowels of compassion from him, how dwelleth the love of God in him? My little children, let us not love in word, neither in tongue; but in deed and in truth" (1 John 3:16-18). Our work in this world is to live for others' good, to bless others, to be hospitable; and frequently it may be only at some inconvenience that we can entertain those who really need our care and the benefit of our society and our homes. Some avoid these necessary burdens.[21]

God's law is the law of love. He has surrounded you with beauty to teach you that you are not placed on earth merely to delve for self, to dig and build, to toil and spin, but to make life bright and joyous and beautiful with the love of Christ—like the flowers, to gladden other lives by the ministry of love.[22]

God's love for mankind was not just expressed in words. In Jesus Christ, God put on human flesh, came to our world, and demonstrated "I love you".

Love is meeting the needs of others.

Love is meeting the needs of others. "Pure religion and undefiled before God and the Father is this, To visit the fatherless and widows in their affliction, and to keep himself unspotted from the world" (James 1:27). If I am a follower of Jesus, a Christian, I am called to follow Jesus' example. "He that saith he abideth in him ought himself also so to walk, even as he walked" (1 John 2:6). "He that loveth not knoweth not God; for God is love" (1 John 4:8). "Beloved, if God so loved us, we ought also to love one another" (1 John 4:11). God explains fasting according to Isaiah 58:5–7. "You humble yourselves by going through the motions of penance, bowing your heads like reeds bending in the wind. You dress in burlap and cover yourselves with ashes. Is this what you call fasting? Do you really think this will please the LORD? No, this is the kind of fasting I want: Free those who are wrongly imprisoned; lighten the burden of those who work for you. Let the oppressed go free, and remove the chains that bind people. Share your food with the hungry, and give shelter to the homeless. Give clothes to those who need them, and do not hide from relatives who need your help" (NLT). What would happen if when you fasted you took the food that you denied yourself and gave it to those who have no food? Fasting is more than just about me and what I want. It is also about meeting the needs of others.

It would not be a great miracle for God to provide the needs described in Matthew 25:35–40. They are a part of His creation. He could send angels to meet their needs. However, the real miracle occurs when He can get me to feed the hungry, take in the stranger, clothe the naked, take care of the sick, give water to the thirsty, and visit those in prison. This would be a manifestation of His power to restore mankind. To get me to act like Him, to love others as He loves, now that would be a *miracle*! "Then said Jesus to them again, Peace be unto you: as my Father hath sent me, even so send I you" (John 20:21). God's ultimate goal for us is to be restored to His likeness. We are saved to serve others.

The real miracle occurs when He can get me to feed the hungry, take in the stranger, clothe the naked, take care of the sick, give water to the thirsty, and visit those in prison.

Chapter 9
Escaped the Corruption

Captivity is the state of being under the control of another or imprisoned.[23] Only those who realize that they are in captivity will ever consider escaping. It is possible to be born with a problem and not realize it is a problem. It seems normal, even fine, and it is all that is ever known. For example, I was born with astigmatism but I thought that I had no problem seeing. I remember being in the classroom sitting on the third row, but I could not see what was written on the blackboard. However, classmates sitting five rows behind me in the same classroom said they could see the blackboard. I thought my classmates were lying. I would think to myself how can they see the blackboard and they are sitting behind me? Consequently, when I put on my first pair of eye glasses I realized what I had been missing. When we realize that we cannot see, then we consider getting our eyes examined. Only those who realize there is a problem will consider and seek an alternative.

"Whereby are given unto us exceeding great and precious promises: that by these ye might be partakers of the divine nature, having escaped the corruption that is in the world through lust" (2 Peter 1:4). God has given us great and precious promises, that by these promises, we may escape the corruption that is in the world through lust. If I see the corruption that is in the world as normal, I have no desire to escape. Sin is abnormal to God and was never intended to be a part of this universe. God created the universe to be sin-free, but sin entered the world through lust. The definition for lust is the desire for that which is forbidden. Like Eve, there are days when we lust for the things that God said is not good for us. However, we can, through God's promises, escape this corruption and choose not to sin.

"For that which I do I allow not: for what I would, that do I not; but what I hate, that do I" (Rom. 7:15). In this passage, Paul acknowledges his frustrations with his own sinful nature. Just like us, he does things that he would not approve of others doing and even does that which he hates. There are things that he should do, that he does not do. I am certain, just like Paul and myself, you have done the same. Sometimes, parents do this with children. There are movies that parents will not allow their children to watch, but the parents will watch them. If the movie is bad, neither the parents nor the children should watch it.

"Now then it is no more I that do it, but sin that dwelleth in me" (Rom. 7:17). Paul recognizes that it is sin that dwells within him, prompting and encouraging him to do that which he would not do. Oh, how do I identify with Paul! What is this sin that dwells in me, that prompts me to sin? This *sin* is selfishness. "The sin which is indulged to the greatest extent, and which separates us from God and produces so many contagious spiritual disorders, is selfishness."[24] I want to do what I want to do. We are born selfish. Parents do not have to teach their children to be selfish. It comes naturally. It is as natural as blinking your eyes. You do not have to tell your eyes to blink; it is a natural response of the body. So it is with selfishness; it is a natural part of our human nature.

"Now if I do that I would not, it is no more I that do it, but sin that dwelleth in me. I find then a law, that, when I would do good, evil is present with me" (Rom. 7:20, 21). Paul continues to address his challenge with sin. In verse 20 he says sin dwells in him. Sin is where he is. He cannot get away from sin. Selfishness is normal, like my poor eyesight without eyeglasses. Paul describes his dilemma of wanting to do good, but not having the ability to perform the good that he desires to do. In verse 21 Paul says, "evil is present with me." So, the problem is with me. "Selfishness is a soul-destroying sin. Under this head comes covetousness, which is idolatry. All things belong to God."[25] My nature naturally is unlike God. I am selfish and God is unselfish. Naturally, I am out of harmony with God and the kingdom of heaven. God is unselfish. He is always giving for the well-being of others. Consequently, He wants to make us like Him. God wants to restore mankind to its original image of His likeness here on this earth.

"For I delight in the law of God after the inward man" (Rom. 7:22). Many people delight in the law of God. They do not want to steal, kill, lie, commit adultery, or participate in false worship, etc. But there are times when our selfish nature will urge us to do things that we believe to be wrong. "The warfare in which we are engaged is largely mental, and the mind that is the most thoroughly trained will do the most acceptable work."[26]

"But I see another law in my members, *warring* against the law of my mind, and bringing me into captivity to the law of sin which is in my members" (Rom. 7:23). (Italics added) What is this *warring* that Paul is speaking about? Yes, there is an internal war going on within mankind. Satan uses the members of my body (my five senses) to wage war against my mind.

There is an internal war going on within mankind. Satan uses the members of my body (my five senses) to wage war against my mind.

There are days when I want to do what is right, but my selfish nature does not want to cooperate, sometimes even keeping me awake at night. There are days when I just sin even without enjoyment, but I do not know how to stop. It's like I am in captivity as Paul mentions in verse 23. If my body cries out for some sinful behavior, my mind seems to just give in, and do what the body is crying out for. "'The carnal mind is enmity against God; for it is not subject to the law of God, neither indeed can be.' Therefore there is a constant warfare between inclination and duty. Inclination too often prevails, and silences the convictions of the Holy Spirit."[27] This is Spiritual Warfare. Satan will use the selfishness of my human nature to drive me to do things I said I would never do. After I do them, my life is filled with pain and regret. Thus the war goes on.

"O wretched man that I am! Who shall deliver me from the body of this death?" (Rom. 7:24). Here Paul describes it as if his own body is working against him. There is a close relationship between mind and body. "There is an intimate relation between the mind and the body, and in order to reach a high standard of moral and intellectual attainment the laws that control our physical being must be heeded."[28] I, like Paul, realize that I am a wretched man and need to be delivered from this body of death.

So what is the answer to this dilemma? "I thank God through Jesus Christ our Lord. So then with the mind I serve the law of God; but with the flesh the law of sin" (Rom. 7:25). Jesus is the answer to the dilemma. Jesus came to deliver me from the selfishness of my own human nature. Luke 4:18 states that Jesus came to set the captives free, and to recover sight to the blind. I am in spiritual captivity to a selfish nature that is unquestionably unlike God, and spiritually blind to Satan's attacks. Therefore, if I follow what my mind knows to be right, God will be happy. But if I follow my selfish, fleshly nature, I will sin.

Paul says in 1 Corinthians 15:31 "...I die daily." Paul declares that daily he had to die to the cravings and desires of his selfish nature, that he might do the will of

God. So when my selfish nature wants something that is not in harmony with the will of God, I should respond to the desires like a dead man. The dead are not manipulated by craving or desires. The dead wait to hear and follow God's voice. Only God has the power to raise the dead, even those dead in trespasses and sin. "And you hath he quickened, who were dead in trespasses and sin" (Eph. 2:1). God has the power to raise even those who have been dead in sin. He can set free those who have been in captivity to a selfish human nature. When we surrender to God the old man will die, and we will no longer be manipulated by the selfish flesh.

"Neither yield ye your members as instruments of unrighteousness unto sin: but yield yourselves unto God, as those that are alive from the dead, and your members as instruments of righteousness unto God" (Rom. 6:13). Here we are admonished to yield ourselves to God. To yield is to relinquish control to another. God requires that we surrender control to Him.

"Lest Satan should get an advantage of us: for we are not ignorant of his devices" (2 Cor. 2:11). God does not want us to be ignorant of Satan's devices. He wants us to be aware of Satan and his tricks. Luke 4:18 states that Jesus came to restore sight to the blind. When our sight is restored, Satan cannot take advantage of us. We realize that it is not safe to follow the promptings of our human, fleshly nature. "Dearly beloved, I beseech you as strangers and pilgrims, abstain from fleshly lusts, which war against the soul" (1 Peter 2:11). There is a war going on against my soul. Satan will use my own body to wage war against me. Satan wants to have me desire the very thing I know is not good for me. "But I keep under my body, and bring it into subjection..." (1

Cor. 9:27). God wants the body to be in subjection and subservient to the mind. The mind is not to be manipulated by the body. As mentioned earlier, God wants us to have the mind of Christ. "And be not conformed to this world: but be ye transformed by the renewing of your mind, that ye may prove what is that good, and acceptable, and perfect, will of God" (Rom. 12:2).

We escape the corruption that is in the world through lust by allowing God to deliver us from the control that our human nature has on our lives; a human nature that is rebellious and self-centered. We naturally want to have our own way. God wants us to surrender to Him and no longer be manipulated by our human nature. He came to set the captives free. He wants to give us a new mind.

Chapter 10
Looking for Benjamin

The spiritual warfare continues as we consider the mission of Christ. "For the Son of man is come to save that which was lost. How think ye? If a man have an hundred sheep, and one of them be gone astray, doth he not leave the ninety and nine, and goeth into the mountains, and seeketh that which is gone astray?" (Matt. 18:11, 12). If one sheep is lost, he leaves the ninety nine in a safe place while he searches for the one that was lost. Why does the shepherd spend time looking for this one sheep? The shepherd looks because the sheep is valuable to the shepherd. This is why the shepherd searches for the one that is lost. He spends time and energy in pursuit of what he values.

Money is valuable in our society. Now if it was money that was lost, with Benjamin Franklin's face on the front of it— a $100 bill—we, too, would search as the shepherd did. Some may say, "It is just a piece of paper, why bother?" My response would be that it is my Benjamin. It doesn't matter if you have other bills of equal value in your wallet, you still look for that one lost Benjamin. The truth of the matter is, we all look for those things we value. If we are this way about lost money, what about lost people—John, Mary, Charles, or Michael? Aren't people much more valuable than money? Jesus says He came to save the lost. He left heaven for lost people. Am I willing to leave everything for the well-being of others?

Jesus says He came to save the lost. He left heaven for lost people. Am I willing to leave everything for the well-being of others?

God sent His son to seek and to save the lost and we are to follow His example. "...As my Father hath sent me, even so send I you" (John 20:21). We are sent to seek and save the lost. "And all things are of God, who hath reconciled us to himself by Jesus Christ, and hath given to us the ministry of reconciliation" (2 Cor. 5:18). Reconciliation is the restoration to Divine favor; atonement. So God has given unto us the ministry of helping others be restored to favor with God. "To wit, that God was in Christ, reconciling the world unto himself, not imputing their trespasses unto them; and hath committed unto us the word of reconciliation. Now then we are ambassadors for Christ, as though God did beseech you by us: we pray you in Christ's stead, be ye reconciled to God" (2 Cor. 5:19, 20). An ambassador, by definition, is: Ambassador 1. A minister of the highest rank sent to a foreign court to represent there his sovereign or country.[29] So God would have us represent Him before others and to assist others to be restored to divine favor. To advance God's kingdom, to arouse those dead in trespasses and sins, to speak to sinners of the healing balm of the Saviour's love,—it is for this that our money should be used. But too often it is used for self-glorification. Instead of being the means of bringing souls to a knowledge of God and Christ, thus calling forth praise and gratitude to the Giver of all good, earthly possessions have been the means of eclipsing the glory of God and obscuring the view of heaven.[30]

If we are going to use our money, means, and finances to bless others, we truly must have a new mind. Naturally, we want to keep all of our resources for ourselves. Therein lies the spiritual warfare, knowing how God would have us live to bless others but so often self does not want to cooperate with God. We sometimes value money more than people. So, God sends His people out into the world as His representatives to portray and display before the world the values of the Kingdom of God and to invite others to abandon the kingdom of this world, then join the Kingdom of God. We are not here for self, but to serve others, and make our Heavenly Father look good. "God's law is the law of love. He has surrounded you with beauty to teach you that you are not placed on, earth merely to delve for self, to dig and build, to toil and spin, but to make life bright and joyous and beautiful with the love of Christ—like the flowers, to gladden other lives by the ministry of love."[31] "Ye are the light of the world. A city that is set on an hill cannot be hid" (Matt. 5:14). A light is placed in a room to help us see. It is to benefit those in the room, not the light itself. A light is used to improve or enhance the quality of the lives of others. Why else put the light in a room? If it refuses to shine, it serves no purpose to the owner. Please let your light shine, that others may be blessed.

As followers of Christ, our lives should be more about seeking lost people than the pursuit of money or prosperity. Jesus was on a mission to bring salvation to a lost world. He was not here to gain worldly riches. Jesus is our example.

Chapter 11
Point of Clarity

God brought the children of Israel out of Egypt. They thought that all they needed was deliverance from Pharaoh and slavery. God shared the commandments with them so that they might realize that they needed more than just deliverance from slavery in Egypt. He wanted them to realize how hopeless and desperate their situation really was without His assistance. When He gave them the commandments, they responded that they would follow them. Upon hearing the people's response, God told the people to return to their tents. They had totally missed what He was trying to share with them. God wanted them to realize that their problem was deeper than deliverance from Egyptian bondage. They were in spiritual bondage as well, and needed to be delivered.

The commandments are the standards that God wants His people to follow. They help us know how to love and behave toward others. They teach us how to love. They show us that without God's intervention, we are helpless and hopeless to love others as we love ourselves.

Of all the commandments, the fourth is most controversial, the most misunderstood, and the most challenging. The Sabbath—what is this all about? The fourth commandment is recorded in Exodus 20:8–11 and in Deuteronomy 5:12–15. The wording in each location is almost the identical in the first three verses. In Exodus 20:11 it states, "For in six days the LORD made heaven and earth, the sea, and all that in them is, and rested the seventh day: wherefore the Lord blessed the sabbath day, and hallowed it." God refers to what He did as the Creator as the reason for keeping the Sabbath. In Deuteronomy 5:15 it reads, "And remember that thou wast a servant in the land of Egypt, and that the LORD thy God brought thee out thence through a mighty hand and by a stretched out arm: therefore the LORD thy God commanded thee to keep the sabbath day." The Israelites were not in Egypt waiting tables and getting tips. They were crying out to God for deliverance from slavery. They longed for the land that God had promised to their forefather Abraham. God stepped in with His mighty hand and brought them out of Egypt.

He was their deliverer from the physical bondage of slavery in Egypt. God refers to what He did—delivering the Israelites from Egypt— as a reason for keeping the Sabbath. Unfortunately, slavery to the Egyptians was not their only problem. The Israelites were slaves to sin. They were slaves to their selfish human nature.

Unfortunately, slavery to the Egyptians was not their only problem. The Israelites were slaves to sin.

Herein lies the problem for the whole human race since the fall in the Garden of Eden. Adam and Eve fell in to sin and it changed them in more ways than we realize. It left them selfish, self-centered and unable to live as God required without His involvement. Mankind can only reproduce after their own kind; therefore, two sinners can only produce a sinner. It was not long after leaving Egypt that their sin problem became very apparent through their worshipping the golden calf, envying Moses' position, adultery, etc. God wanted to deliver them from the sin which was ruling and ruining their lives. Sin was a cruel dictator, there were days they would act worse than the heathen nations around them. Some days they lived like they did not know God at all. They were content with physical deliverance from Egypt, but God wanted them to have so much more; spiritual deliverance and restoration to His image. He wanted to restore them to His likeness.

After they were restored to His image, God wanted to set them out before the world as an example of what was available to other nations should they choose to follow the true God. In Isaiah He makes it clear that He wanted them to be a light for the Gentiles.

"I the LORD have called thee in righteousness, and will hold thine hand, and will keep thee, and give thee for a covenant of the people, for a light of the Gentiles" (Isa. 42:6). A light removes the darkness from a room and enhances the quality of the room. Israel was to be God's light to the Gentiles. They were to show the nations how to live according to God's desire.

The Sabbath was to be a reminder of their spiritual deliverance. In Deuteronomy 5:15 God reminds the Israelites that they were slaves in Egypt and that He delivered them. He reminded them that they were delivered physically through His mighty hand. Spiritually, they were delivered by His out-stretched arms. What happened to Jesus' arms at Calvary? His arms were stretched out. Why were His arms stretched out? They provided deliverance from slavery to sin. The Sabbath was to be a weekly reminder of the One who had redeemed them from slavery physically and spiritually. Each week they would remember their Deliverer. It is sad to say, many were only interested in physical deliverance. They thought they were fine, spiritually. With that attitude, they fell spiritually on their faces over and over again.

God has recorded Israel's history to serve as warning to others. "Now all these things happened unto them for ensamples: and they are written for our admonition, upon whom the ends of the world are come. Wherefore let him that thinketh he standeth take heed lest he fall. There hath no temptation taken you but such as is common to man: but God is faithful, who will not suffer you to be tempted above that ye are able; but will with the temptation also make a way to escape, that ye may be able to bear it" (1 Cor. 10:11–13). It is easy for me to think that physical deliverance is enough, but that was also Israel's point of view. God provides a way of escape, from any and all temptations, but I, like Israel, some days do not want to escape. I only want God to change my situation. I do not want God to change me. God wants to restore His people physically and spiritually. The Sabbath is a reminder of God's out-stretched arms and that both physical and spiritual deliverance are available. In Luke 4:18 Jesus says He came, "...to preach deliverance to the captives, and recovering of sight to the blind..."

I only want God to change my situation. I do not want God to change me.

Who is in captivity? Mankind is in captivity to a sinful nature. To be clear, mankind needs deliverance from his selfish human nature that is at enmity with God. The Sabbath is to be a weekly reminder that we can be delivered from selfishness. God can set us free from captivity to our sinful nature.

Chapter 12
The Question

What does the previous chapter's discussion about the Israelites have to do with us today? In Exodus 20:8–11, the Sabbath was given to remind God's people of their Creator. In Deuteronomy 5:12–15, the Sabbath was given to remind God's people of their Deliverer. God was their Savior from slavery in Egypt. Here God was offering both physical and spiritual freedom. Not just removal of physical bondage, but to remove the selfishness of their human nature. Selfishness is the engine that drives man to perform sinful acts. Selfishness is what makes us so unfit for heaven; which is the ultimate *Promised Land*.

All sin is selfishness. Satan's first sin was a manifestation of selfishness. He sought to grasp power, to exalt self. A species of insanity led him to seek to supersede God. And the temptation that led Adam to sin, was Satan's declaration that it was possible for man to attain to something more than he already enjoyed—possible for him to be as God Himself. The sowing of seeds of selfishness in the human heart was the first result of the entrance of sin into the world. God desires every one to understand the evil of selfishness, and to cooperate with Him in guarding the human family against its terrible, deceptive power. The design of the gospel is to confront this evil by means of remedial missionary work, and to destroy its destructive power by establishing enterprises of benevolence... Sin has extinguished the love that God placed in man's heart. The work of the church is to rekindle this love. The church is to cooperate with God by uprooting selfishness from the human heart, placing in its stead the benevolence that was in man's heart in his original state of perfection. [32]

The temptation that led Adam to sin, was Satan's declaration that it was possible for man to attain to something more than he already enjoyed—possible for him to be as God Himself.

How was the Sabbath supposed to address man's selfish nature? "Six days shalt thou labour, and do all thy work: But the seventh day is the sabbath of the LORD thy God: in it thou shalt not do any work, thou, nor thy son, nor thy daughter, thy manservant, nor thy maidservant, nor thy cattle, nor thy stranger that is within thy gates" (Ex. 20:9, 10). The command clearly states that mankind was to dedicate six days to their employment. They had six days to address all their work. Strong's Concordance defines the word "work" in Exodus 20:10 as, "ministry; generally employment (never servile) or work (abstractly or concretely)". So what's the point? "And man also has a work to perform on this day (the Sabbath). The necessities of life must be attended to, the sick must be cared for, and the wants of the needy must be supplied. He will not be held guiltless who neglects to relieve suffering on the Sabbath. God's holy rest day was made for man, and acts of mercy are in perfect harmony with its intent."[33] (Clarification added.) Man should dedicate six days to his work or employment, but never stop serving others. On the Sabbath, because I am not doing my work, I have more time to serve others. More time to help others experience freedom and deliverance from whatever has burdened their lives. Those that are experiencing life challenges will have a happy Sabbath because I showed up and helped them experience relief, and I asked for nothing in return. During these hours, man should stop focusing on his personal well-being and seek to be a blessing or benefit to his fellow man.

"For even hereunto were ye called: because Christ also suffered for us, leaving us an example, that ye should follow his steps" (1 Peter 2:23). Christ gives us the example of God's ideal of Sabbath observance and we are to follow in His steps. What did Jesus do on the Sabbath? In Luke 4:16 it reads, "And he came to Nazareth, where he had been brought up: and, as his custom was, he went into the synagogue on the sabbath day, and stood up for to read." Christ went to church and got involved in the service on the Sabbath. What else did Jesus do on the Sabbath? He provided deliverance to the captives—people in local communities who were in unfortunate situations.

❖ Luke 6: 6–11 The man with a withered hand

❖ Luke 13:10–17 The woman bent over for eighteen years

❖ Luke 14:1–6 The man with the dropsy

❖ John 5:1–14 The man with an infirmity thirty-eight years

❖ John 9:1–16 The man born blind

Jesus spent time on the Sabbath doing good for others. Each of these people in the above examples experienced some form of deliverance on the Sabbath. Therefore, the Sabbath was a happy experience for each of them because of how Jesus kept the Sabbath.

Jesus spent time on the Sabbath doing good for others.

"Heaven's work never ceases, and men should never rest from doing good. The Sabbath is not intended to be a period of useless inactivity. The law forbids secular labor on the rest day of the Lord; the toil that gains a livelihood must cease; no labor for worldly pleasure or profit is lawful upon that day; but as God ceased His labor of creating, and rested upon the Sabbath and blessed it, so man is to leave the occupations of his daily life, and devote those sacred hours to healthful rest, to worship, and to holy deeds."[34] What would happen if we followed Jesus example? We go to church and then go into the local community to extend relief to those who are burdened, like Jesus, asking for nothing in return. Consequently, we should just be thankful that God has allowed us to play a part in blessing someone else. "Then said Jesus to them again, Peace be unto you: as my Father hath sent me, even so send I you" (John 20:21).

Could it be possible to embrace the Sabbath based on creation, but to overlook the deliverance in Deuteronomy 5:15? We can go to church, then spend the rest of the day serving ourselves. The Sabbath is to be a day of deliverance. God delivered us, now He wants to use us to convey deliverance to others. The Sabbath gives us an excellent opportunity to demonstrate God's power to deliver from bondage and slavery to a selfish nature. We once lived and served only ourselves. God has delivered us from that. Now the Sabbath is a weekly reminder that we are in this world to be a blessing to others. "Selfishness is a soul-destroying sin. Under this head comes covetousness, which is idolatry. All things belong to God. All the prosperity we enjoy is the result of divine beneficence."[35] Selfishness no longer rules or dictates our lives. "Let not sin therefore reign in your mortal body, that ye should obey it in the lusts thereof" (Rom. 6:12).

Jesus clashed with the religious leaders of his day because He utilized the Sabbath hours as a time to

enhance and improve the quality of life of others. Jesus
spent this time helping others.

> All may find something to do...Millions upon
> millions of human souls ready to perish,
> bound in chains of ignorance and sin, have
> never so much as heard of Christ's love for
> them. Were our condition and theirs to be
> reversed, what would we desire them to do
> for us? All this, so far as lies in our power, we
> are under the most solemn obligation to do
> for them. Christ's rule of life, by which every
> one of us must stand or fall in the judgment,
> is, "Whatsoever ye would that men should do
> to you, do ye even so to them." The Saviour
> has given His precious life in order to estab-
> lish a church capable of caring for sorrowful,
> tempted souls...It is because this work is
> neglected that so many young disciples never
> advance beyond the mere alphabet of Chris-
> tian experience. The light which was glow-
> ing in their own hearts when Jesus spoke to
> them, "Thy sins be forgiven thee," they might
> have kept alive by helping those in need.[36]

*The Pharisees kept to themselves
on the Sabbath doing nothing for
anyone but themselves.
The conflict was not what day was
the Sabbath, but what to do
during the Sabbath hours.*

The Pharisees kept to themselves on the Sabbath doing nothing for anyone but themselves. The conflict was not what day was the Sabbath, but what to do during the Sabbath hours. Should I help others or help myself? Should I stay home and keep to myself or go out into the community and help others experience deliverance? What would Jesus do? That is the question—what is Jesus calling me to do? Is He calling me to continue to serve myself or to embrace His example and serve others?

Chapter 13
Restoration

"The church is God's fortress, His city of refuge, which He holds in a revolted world."[30] The definition for revolt is: 1. to turn away; to abandon or reject something; specifically, to turn away, or shrink, with abhorrence. 2. Hence, to be faithless; to desert one party or leader for another; especially, to renounce allegiance or subjection; to rise against a government; to rebel. 3. To be disgusted, shocked, or grossly offended; hence, to feel nausea; -- with at; as, the stomach revolts at such food; his nature revolts at cruelty.[37] Today the world has staged a revolt against God. It has turned away from the Bible and its teachings. The world has abandoned loving others as one loves him or herself, which is what God teaches in His Word. Some people use religion as a means to financially advance themselves in this life. They do not promote the principles of God, to love others as one loves him or herself, instead they promote self. Seemingly, they are unaware that we are not here to promote self; we are here to promote the kingdom of God. This world is a penal colony for sinners. Only those who allow God to put them through spiritual rehab will make it into His kingdom.

This world is a penal colony for sinners. Only those who allow God to put them through spiritual rehab will make it into His kingdom.

Through selfishness, sin has changed the human race into cold and unkind beings. God is convinced that He can restore this fallen race to His image. He will demonstrate to the universe, through His love, His compassion, and His forgiveness, His true character. Satan will be seen as the liar that he truly is. "Then every knee will bow and every tongue confess that Jesus is Lord to the glory of God" Phil 2:10. "The church is the repository of the riches of the grace of Christ; and through the church will eventually be made manifest, even to 'the principalities and powers in heavenly places,' the final and full display of the love of God."[38]

God's plan has always been not just to forgive mankind but to restore him. Please do not settle for forgiveness only. Forgiveness is good, but God wants to take you from good to great. From forgiven to restoration. From the love of self to selfless love for others.

From a "me first" mind set to an "others first" state of mind. He wants you to have the mind of Christ. "Let this mind be in you, which was also in Christ Jesus" (Phil. 2:5). Note the word "let". God wants to make the mind of Christ in us a reality, the question is do we want to let Him do it.

"Forasmuch then as Christ hath suffered for us in the flesh, arm yourselves likewise with the same mind: for he that hath suffered in the flesh hath ceased from sin" (1 Peter 4:1). Christ was willing to let His flesh suffer before He would do anything displeasing to His Father in heaven. If we are not armed with the mind of Christ, we are in a spiritual war and totally unarmed and unprepared for real spiritual warfare. "For the grace of God that bringeth salvation hath appeared to all men, teaching us that, denying ungodliness and worldly lusts, we should live soberly, righteously, and godly, in this present world" (Titus 2:11, 12). This "grace of God that brings salvation", according to verse 12, is to be "teaching us". What is the grace of God teaching us? The grace of God is teaching us to say no to selfishness and worldly lusts, and that we should live soberly, righteously, and godly, in this present world. We are to live soberly, righteously and godly, not in some world to come but in this present world. While the rest of the world is still in rebellion, God calls you to live righteous, sober, and godly today by His grace.

How is it possible? "...Because the love of God is shed abroad in our hearts by the Holy Ghost which is given unto us" (Rom. 5:5). The Holy Ghost puts God's love in your heart. "At the cost of infinite sacrifice and suffering, Christ has provided for us every essential to success in the Christian warfare. The Holy Spirit brings power that enables man to overcome. It is through the agency of the Spirit that the government of Satan is to be subdued. It is the Spirit that convinces of sin, and, with the consent of the human being, expels sin from the heart. The mind is then brought under a new law,—the royal law of liberty."[39] "It is by the Spirit that the heart is made pure. Through the Spirit the believer becomes a partaker of the divine nature. Christ has given his Spirit as a divine power to overcome all hereditary and cultivated tendencies to evil, and to impress his own character upon the church."[40] Everything God wants to accomplish in and through your life He is able to complete, with your consent and operation. "Being confident of this very thing, that He which hath begun a good work in you will perform it until the day of Jesus Christ" (Phil. 1:6).

It is the Spirit that convinces of sin, and, with the consent of the human being, expels sin from the heart. The mind is then brought under a new law,—the royal law of liberty.

God chose Mary to be the vessel that would carry and give birth to the Messiah. The only thing that He needed from Mary was her consent. God had everything necessary to put divinity into humanity. He would bring out of her a new life; a new creature. What will He do with your consent if you allow Him to have His way in your life? What would be possible with your consent? In

Luke 1:37 we are told with God, nothing shall be impossible.

Restoration is His goal for mankind, including you. "And He that sat upon the throne said, Behold, I make all things new. And he said unto me, Write: for these words are true and faithful" (Rev. 21:5). Please surrender to God, that He may prepare us for the kingdom.

References

1. White, E. G., *Testimonies for the Church*, Vol. 3
   p. 82, par. 3

2. White, E. G., *Spiritual Gifts*, Vol. 4b, p. 124:2

3. White, E. G., *In Heavenly Places*, p. 69:2

4. White, E. G., *Review and Herald*, October 11, 1892,
   par. 8

5. White, E. G., *Review and Herald*, May 19, 1904,
   par. 3

6. Ibid, par. 5

7. White, E. G., *Signs of the Times*, February 16, 1882,
   par. 3

8. White, E. G., *Steps to Christ*, p. 43, par. 3

9. White, E. G., *Signs of the Times*, August 23, 1905, par. 4, 5

10. White, E. G., *Signs of the Times*, November 30, 1891, par. 11

11. White, E. G., *Signs of the Times*, September 7, 1891, par. 4

12. White, E. G., *Steps to Christ*, p. 78

13. Ibid, p. 79

14. Ibid, p. 79

15. White, E. G., *Testimonies for the Church*, Vol. 2 p. 645

16. White, E. G., *Desire of Ages*, p. 825

17. White, E. G., *Thoughts From the Mount of Blessing*, p. 97

18. White, E. G., *Testimonies for the Church*, Vol. 3 pp. 512-513

19. White, E. G., *Christ's Object Lessons*, p. 340

20. White, E. G., *Testimonies for the Church*, Vol. 3, p. 511

21. White, E. G., *Testimonies for the Church*, Vol. 2, p. 645

22. White, E. G., *Thoughts From the Mount of Blessings*, p. 97

23. *Webster's Revised Unabridged Dictionary*, 1913 edition

24. White, E. G., *Testimony Treasures*, Vol 1, p. 206

25. Ibid, p. 554

26. White, E. G., *Signs of the Times*, September 7, 1891, par. 4

27. White, E. G., *Signs of the Times*, February 16, 1882, par. 3

28. White, E. G., *Patriarch and Prophets*, p. 601

29. *The Collaborative International Dictionary of English* v.0.48, www.Dict.org/bin/Dict

30. White, E. G., Counsels on Stewardship, p. 223

31. White, E. G., *Thoughts From the Mount of Blessings*, p. 97

32. White, E. G., *Workers' Bulletin*, September 9, 1902, par. 3, 5

33. White, E. G., Desire of Ages, p. 207

34. Ibid, p.207

35. White, E. G., *Testimonies for the Church*, Vol. 1, p. 554, par. 1

36. White, E. G., *Desire of Ages*, p. 640, par. 3

37. *The Collaborative International Dictionary of English* v.0.48, www.Dict.org/bin/Dict

38. White, E. G., *The Acts of the Apostles*, p. 9, par. 1

39. White, E. G., *Review and Herald*, May 19, 1904, par. 5

40. Ibid, par. 3

We invite you to view the complete
selection of titles we publish at:

www.TEACHServices.com

Please write or email us your praises, reactions, or
thoughts about this or any other book we publish at:

TEACH Services, Inc.
P U B L I S H I N G
www.TEACHServices.com • (800) 367-1844

P.O. Box 954
Ringgold, GA 30736

Info@TEACHServices.com

TEACH Services, Inc., titles may be purchased in bulk for
educational, business, fund-raising, or sales promotional use.
For information, please e-mail:

BulkSales@TEACHServices.com

Finally if you are interested in seeing
your own book in print, please contact us at

publishing@TEACHServices.com

We would be happy to review your manuscript for free.

www.ingramcontent.com/pod-product-compliance
Lightning Source LLC
Chambersburg PA
CBHW060554100426
42742CB00013B/2549